ISBN 0 85116 220 7

THE FIRESIDE BOOK

A picture and a poem for every mood
chosen by

DAVID HOPE

Printed and Published by
D. C. THOMSON & CO. LTD.,
185 Fleet Street, London EC4A 2HS.

INVITATION

THERE is no reason I can see
    Why anyone should visit me.
My house is very badly run—
I sit too often in the sun.
My garden's full of wicked weeds,
And seldom gets the care it needs!

But at the moment there is treasure,
In which the caller may find pleasure,
The apple trees are bravely dressed
With pale pink blossom at its best;
And, in addition, you can see
Three kittens and a lilac tree.

These will not last—the kits will grow,
And apple-blossom fall like snow.
I do not wish to ape my betters
And write you importuning letters,
But, if you're passing, come and see
The kittens and the lilac tree.

Kate Bone

THE LINNET

UPON this leafy bush
   With thorns and roses in it,
Flutters a thing of light,
   A twittering linnet,
And all the throbbing world
   Of dew and sun and air
By this small parcel of life
   Is made more fair;
As if each bramble-spray
   And mounded gold-wreathed furze,
Harebell and little thyme,
   Were only hers;
As if this beauty and grace
   Did to one bird belong,
And, at a flutter of wing,
   Might vanish in song.

Walter de la Mare

WINDFALLS

AFTER the storm had passed,
   The moon rose,
Silvering the orchard trees,
And underneath their
Leafy canopies,
The windfalls lay,
Bright scattered balls of silver
In the grass,
Wet from the rain under the
Silvered trees.
An owl took wing from a great oak,
Hooting by moonshine, to pass
On his wide-winged way
Through the bright night,
And, scattered in the grass,
Like Christmas baubles,
Quiet the windfalls lay.

Aileen E. Passmore

TO AN OLD TEAPOT

NOW from the dust of half-forgotten things,
  You rise to haunt me at the year's Spring-
    cleaning
And bring to memory dim imaginings
  Of mystic meaning.

No old-timer potter handled you, I ween,
  Nor yet were you of gold or silver molten;
No Derby stamp, nor Worcester, can be seen,
  Nor Royal Doulton.

You never stood to grace the princely board
  Of monarchs in some Oriental palace.
Your lid is chipped, your chubby side is scored
  As if in malice.

I hesitate to say it, but your spout
  Is with unhandsome rivets held together—
Mute witnesses of treatment meted out
  In regions nether.

O patient sufferer of many bumps!
  I ask it gently—shall the dustbin hold you?
And will the dust-heap, with its cabbage stumps,
  At last enfold you?

It ought. And yet with gentle hands I place
  You with my priceless Delft and Dresden china,
For sake of one who loved your homely face
  In days diviner.

Fay Inchfawn

B

AS I WENT A-WALKING . . .

AS I went a-walking on Lavender Hill,
    O, I met a darling in frock and frill;
And she looked at me shyly, with eyes of blue:
" Are you going a-walking? Then take me too!"

So we strolled to the field where the cowslips grow,
And we played and we played for an hour or so;
Then we climbed to the top of the old park wall,
And the darling she threaded a cowslip ball.

Then we played again, till I said, " My dear,
This pain in my side, it has grown severe;
I ought to have told you I'm past three score,
And I fear that I scarcely can play any more!"

But the darling she answered, " O no! O no!
You must play—you must play—I shan't let you go!"
—And I woke with a start and a sigh of despair
And I found myself safe in my Grandfather's chair!

Austin Dobson

MY HEARTH

A GOD, a god sits on my hearth,
  Laughs and plays with sober mirth,
Sings a small song, merry and wild,
As a bird might or a child.

Strayed here from some Olympian hill,
This god is rose and daffodil
Yet boils my kettle, cooks my dish,
Gives savour to the meats and fish.

I stretch my chilly hands above
And like my dog he fawns in love,
Licks at me with a playful tongue
And frisks, a bright thing, merry and young.

And yet so great a god is he,
You shall approach him on your knee,
Lest that his lightnings teach you awe,
This Burning Bush that Moses saw.

This holy one stays with me still,
Singing his small song merry and shrill,
And hath so many things to do,
There is no time to grieve or rue.

For the great state he hath forgone,
The Lord Sun's dear companion,
Who toils and plays upon my hearth,
Nor yet forgets his starry birth.

Katharine Tynan

THE WINDMILL

THE green corn waving in the dale,
　　The ripe grass waving on the hill:
I lean across the paddock pale
　　And gaze upon the giddy mill.

Its hurtling sails a mighty sweep
　　Cut thro' the air: with rushing sound
Each strikes in fury down the steep,
　　Rattles, and whirls in chase around.

Beside his sacks the miller stands
　　On high within the open door:
A book and pencil in his hands,
　　His grist and meal he reckoneth o'er.

His tireless merry slave the wind
　　Is busy with his work today:
From whencesoe'er, he comes to grind;
　　He hath a will and knows the way.

He gives the creaking sails a spin,
　　The circling millstones faster flee,
The shuddering timbers groan within,
　　And down the shoot the meal runs free.

The miller giveth him no thanks,
　　And doth not much his work o'erlook:
He stands beside the sacks, and ranks
　　The figures in his dusty book.

Robert Bridges

ON EASTNOR KNOLL

SILENT are the woods, and the dim green
    boughs are
Hushed in the twilight: yonder in the path through
The apple orchard, is a tired plough-boy
    Calling the cows home.

A bright white star blinks, the pale moon
    rounds, but
Still the red, lurid wreckage of the sunset
Smoulders in smoky fire, and burns on
    The misty hill-tops.

Ghostly it grows, and darker, the burning
Fades into smoke, and now the gusty oaks are
A silent army of phantoms thronging
    A land of shadows.

John Masefield

ASK AND HAVE

"OH, 'tis time I should talk to your mother,
    Sweet Mary," says I.
" Oh, don't talk to my mother," says Mary,
Beginning to cry:
" For my mother says men are deceivers,
And never, I know, will consent;
She says girls in a hurry who marry,
At leisure repent."

" Then, suppose I would talk to your father,
Sweet Mary," says I.
" Oh, don't talk to my father," says Mary,
Beginning to cry:
" For my father he loves me so dearly,
He'll never consent I should go—
If you talk to my father," says Mary,
" He'll surely say, ' No.' "

"Then how shall I get you, my jewel?
Sweet Mary," says I;
"If your father and mother's so cruel,
Most surely I'll die."
"Oh, never say die, dear," says Mary;
"A way now to save you I see:
Since my parents are both so contrary—
You'd better ask me!"

Samuel Lover

IF THOU MUST LOVE ME

IF thou must love me, let it be for nought
  Except for love's sake only. Do not say,
" I love her for her smile—her look—her way
Of speaking gently,—for a trick of thought
That falls in well with mine, and certes brought
A sense of pleasant ease on such a day "—
For these things in themselves, Beloved, may
Be changed, or change for thee—and love, so
    wrought,
May be unwrought so. Neither love me for
Thine own dear pity's wiping my cheeks dry:
A creature might forget to weep, who bore
Thy comfort long, and lose thy love thereby!
But love me for love's sake, that evermore
Thou may'st love on, through love's eternity.

Elizabeth Barrett Browning

PLAYFORD

UPON a hill-side green and fair
   The happy traveller sees
White cottages peep here and there
   Between the tufts of trees;
With a white farm-house on the brow,
And an old grey Hall below
   With moat and garden round;
And on a Sabbath wandering near
Through all the quiet place you hear
   A Sabbath-breathing sound:
The church-bell slowly swinging
   In an old grey tower above
The wooded hill, where birds are singing
   In the deep quiet of the grove.
And when the bell shall cease to ring,
And the birds no longer sing,
And the grasshopper is heard no more,
   A sound of praise, of prayer,
   Rises along the air,
Like the sea murmur from a distant shore.

Bernard Barton

FAIRY STORY

IF meadow-grass can turn to milk,
　　And glassy ice to water,
If worms can fashion golden silk
To clothe a royal daughter,
If caterpillars, weaving, first,
A chrysalis, that's made to burst,
Can nibble out their way (head first)
As butterflies, more splendid
Than ladies who surround a throne—
Then who would make the silly moan
That fairy tales are ended?

If tiny wheelwrights of the dawn,
Their silver threads unreeling,
Can decorate a garden's lawn
With wheels (too fine for wheeling),
If speckled eggs, as petal-frail
As caskets in a fairy tale,
Can hold a chorus, that will scale
The skies, in rapture chanting,
Then who on earth will dare to say
That magic was for yesterday,
And not for our enchanting?

Barbara Euphan Todd

LONELY PLACES

MOURN for the lost and lonely places
 Filled with the wind's thin tune
And the haunting cry of a night bird
 Under a sailing moon.

Weep for all the plundered places
 And everything they meant
Of joy and beauty, peace, repose
 And life's replenishment.

Remember them, the lonely places
 Where now the cities beat.
Remember them for they lie asleep
 Beneath your hastening feet.

Mary C. Marshall

THE GOLDEN BOWL

THE golden bowl in beauty glows and glows!
   The golden bowl of old Kakiemon!
Whose cunning wrought these dragon
   shapes upon
Flower of the kiku that their coils disclose.
And I have set it where the sunlight flows
In from an English garden all day long,
Made murmurous with sound of birds in song,
And scented with the lavender and rose.
And yet it is not mine! The distant East,
The Country of the Sun has thought to fill
Its heart with dreams; until it glows the more
In memory of a rich, and bygone feast,
Longing to brim with the warm sake, still
Pressed to the lips of some dead Emperor.

K. V. Chevis

APRIL

THE clouds are hanging out to dry,
  Like carded wool across the sky.

The warm bright sap is rising now,
In every trunk and twisted bough.

A calf tried out his wobbly legs,
As stiff and new as wooden pegs.

Wild ducks are swimming in the sloughs
A meadow lark broadcasts the news.

The crocuses in serried ranks
Are marching down the river banks.

A baby lamb like a stuffed toy,
Is following a little boy.

The lilacs have begun to show,
A happy robin told me so.

A farmer in his faded clothes
Is sowing wheat in long brown rows.

And all the lovely countryside
Has put on Beauty like a bride.

Edna Jaques

THE HAPPY ANGLER

HAVE you ever been a-fishing
  With your rod, and hook and line?
As a means of recreation
  All declare it superfine.
You may bid farewell to trouble,
  All your cares you may resign
If you only go a-fishing
  With your rod, and hook and line.

Though at times your luck's uncertain,
  And your chances are but small,
Sure you never mind the bother—
  Here in happy Donegal;
O! the pleasure and excitement,
  Yea, the tingle down your spine,
When you've caught a silvery salmon
  Playing fast with rod and line.

Some are keen on golf and tennis,
  Some inclined the hounds to follow;
Devotees have each in plenty,
  Angling truly beats them hollow.
Good old kindly Isaak Walton,
  You've explored a golden mine,
Yielding health and wealth and pleasure
  With your rod, and hook and line.

Each one of the genus homo
  Must at times be free from care;
Sound in mind and sound in body
  Is a blessing all should share.
This to get and hold securely,
  Plans are plotted, I opine,
My advice is go a-fishing
  With your rod, and hook and line.

John Clinton O'Boyce

GOOD-NIGHT

KISS Susannah gently,
   For she has closed her eyes,
To dream of swings and slippery slides,
Shopping trips and cycle rides.
So kiss Susannah gently tonight.

Kiss Susannah quickly,
For she is going to sleep,
To dream of Bun and Teddy Bear,
And washing Dolly's long blond hair.
So kiss Susannah quickly tonight.

Kiss Susannah softly,
For she is far away,
With Jack and Jill and Goldilocks,
New red shoes and party frocks.
So kiss Susannah softly tonight.

Marion Elliott

THE ROADSIDE PINES

WE paused beneath the shadow of the pines.
　　'Twas very still, no breeze their branches
　　stirred.
Only the sweet, rare twittering of a bird
Spoke, faintly heard.

Silent they stood—most grave and calm;
Hearkening the benediction strong
Of unseen angels, and the triumph song
Roll heaven along.

High priests we deemed them, serving at a shrine.
They draw a blessing down as they adored.
Their secret balm of peace was softly poured
On hearts restored.

Ethel L. Fowler

BEES

BEES are all-wise,
They know
Who's born, who dies.
The country people tell them everything
And the news travels swiftly, wing to wing,
Until it reaches her who broods, wings furled,
At the still centre of that humming world.

They say the night that Farmer Lintott died
The hives were restless all the dark hours through.
He was a good old man. He grew
Apples whose names are all forgotten since,
Medlar and mulberry too and yellow quince.

Each winter through he tended well his hives,
At end of summer took the flower-show prize
With his thick combs of fragrant honey.
He is gone now and with him all his line—
The son was killed in 1939—
New people at the farm with modern ways,
Noisy machinery and poison-sprays
And smart town tricks of making money,
And yet their apple-harvest does not thrive.
Bees are all-wise,
They know
Who's born, who dies.

L. E. Brodie

THE EXPEDITION

WHEN I was quite a little girl
    I would go and shop with Nurse.
Fidgetting I'd twist and twirl
    Till she let me hold her purse.

Best I liked the draper's shop
    With its " tram-line " out of range,
Eagerly I watched it stop,
    A wooden ball brought back our change.

The grocer's was exciting too,
    Biscuits in big tins I'd see,
Sugar in thick bags of blue,
    Canisters of fragrant tea.

The dairy-shop had picture tiles
    Of cows in meadows, sheaves of corn,
The dairy girls with dimpled smiles
    Sold butter-pats as fresh as morn.

The chemist was mysterious
    With splendid coloured bottles. Still
It made me feel too serious,
    Made me think of being ill.

The welcome baker lay ahead,
    Cottage loaves and hot meat pies,
Sponge fingers, men of gingerbread,
    Saffron buns all rich with spice.

Home at last in autumn dusk,
    Shutters closing on the day,
Burning leaves smelt sweet as musk,
    Toast for tea, then happy play.

Rosemary Glubb

IN THE EMBERS

BY the flickering light of a fading fire,
    We sit and dream of an old desire.
Though we know not why, there is something then
That fetches the old things back again
And gazing deep in the dying flames
We think of faces, remember names.
No land is far in the firelight's glow,
And it isn't so long to the long ago.

There are nights we knew that have slipped away,
Like a starlit sky at the dawn of day.
There are days we knew that have westward
    passed,
For not even the day itself can last.
We think our days and nights are done,
With the morning star, and the evening sun,
But when we sit in the firelight here
The past returns, and the loved comes near.

There are things we know that we thought forgot,
For the mind forgets, but the heart does not.
We shall often sit by the fire like this,
We shall hear a voice, and shall feel a kiss,
We leave old homes, and we lose old friends,
We have a joy, and it seems to end.
But they all come back when the new things tire,
By the flickering light of a fading fire.

Anon.

ALL THAT'S PAST

VERY old are the woods;
    And the buds that break
Out of the briar's boughs,
    When March winds wake,
So old with their beauty are—
    Oh, no man knows
Through what wild centuries
    Roves back the rose.

Very old are the brooks;
    And the rills that rise
When snow sleeps cold beneath
    The azure skies
Sing such a history
    Of come and gone,
Their every drop is as wise
    As Solomon.

Very old are we men;
    Our dreams are tales
Told in dim Eden
    By Eve's nightingales;
We wake and whisper awhile,
    But, the day gone by,
Silence and sleep like fields
    Of amaranth lie.

Walter de la Mare

E

THE NIGHTINGALE NEAR THE HOUSE

HERE is the soundless cypress on the lawn:
  It listens, listens. Taller trees beyond
Listen. The moon at the unruffled pond
  Stares. And you sing, you sing.

That star-enchanted song falls through the air
From lawn to lawn down terraces of sound,
Darts in white arrows on the shadowed ground;
  While all the night you sing.

My dreams are flowers to which you are a bee,
As all night I listen, and my brain
Receives your song, then loses it again
  In moonlight on the lawn.

Now is your voice a marble high and white,
Then like a mist on fields of paradise;
Now is a raging fire, then is like ice,
  Then breaks, and it is dawn.

Harold Monro

THE SHIP'S BELL

ON cliffs against the sky
   I stood with a cedar tree
That grew the way of the wind
   And looked down on the sea.

A ship was passing near
   The coast; I could not tell
From lights lost in the mist—
   But I heard a ship's bell.

Above the sea on the rocks
   And the night closing around,
Above the wind on the cliffs—
   A brave, lonely sound!

Fading out to the vast
   Where the late splendours fell,
Muffled and slow from the mist,
   The sound of a ship's bell!

Glenn Ward Dresbach

THE FARM

L O! the sun is o'er the hilltop,
  Lo! the morning breaketh clear;
Merry sounds of mirth and labour
  Waken in the farmyard near.

There the cock sits on the barn door
  Crowing merrily and loud,
And his crimson feathers glisten
  As he shakes his pinions proud.

And the brown hen walks below him
  Picking grains up from the floor;
Bring the fresh egg, bring it quickly
  From the nest behind the door.

With the spade across his shoulder
  To the field the workman goes,
While the watchdog, his work over,
  Seeks the kennel for repose.

'Tis the idle that grow weary,
  Gaily rings each busy sound,
'Tis a pleasure to be active,
  There's a joy in labour found.

And I feel my blood run freer,
  And I own it, kind and good,
That to man the law was given:
  He must work to win his food.

Cecil Frances Alexander

THE WILD FLOWER GARDEN

ALL about the countryside
 God's garden grows—
Ragged Robin, buttercup
 And sweet dog-rose,
Daisy, pansy, meadow-sweet,
 Orchids and violet blue.
All about the countryside
 They blow for me and you.

There's primrose and daffodil,
 Bluebell and thyme,
Silver catkins, hawthorn,
 Blossom of the lime,
Heather on the moorland,
 Blue holly by the sea,
All in God's garden,
 Grow for you and me.

Thora Stowell

THE GIRLS OF DONEGAL

I HAVE met with many a bonny lass
    In Antrim and in Down,
I have seen the Wicklow beauties
    And the swells of Dublin town.
But still I never will forget
    Those girls demure and tall,
Those blue-eyed girls, those dark-eyed girls,
    The girls of Donegal.

I have met them in the market,
    I have met them at the fair,
Those sweet and smiling colleens that
    You'll seldom meet elsewhere.
I'll ne'er forget those happy nights
    When, at a Gaeltacht ball,
I tripped the light fantastic toe
    With girls of Donegal.

I'm now three thousand miles away,
    But soon I'll cease to roam,
I'll wed my darling sweetheart and
    We'll settle down back home.
I meet with Yankee beauties here
    Whose charms are far from small,
But none so fair as can compare
    With girls from Donegal.

Anonymous

THE RUN OF THE DOWNS

THE Weald is good, the Downs are best—
   I'll give you the run of 'em, East to West.
Beachy Head and Winddoor Hill,
They were once and they are still.
Firle, Mount Caburn and Mount Harry
Go back as far as sums'll carry.
Ditchling Beacon and Chanctonbury Ring,
They have looked on many a thing,
And what those two have missed between 'em,
I reckon Truleigh Hill has seen 'em.
Highden, Bignor and Duncton Down
Knew Old England before the Crown.
Linch Down, Treyford and Sunwood
Knew old England before the Flood;
And when you end on the Hampshire side—
Butser's old as Time and Tide.
   The Downs are sheep, the Weald is corn,
   You be glad you are Sussex born!

Rudyard Kipling

IN DORSET DEAR

IN Dorset Dear they're making hay
  In just the old West Country way.
With fork and rake and old-time gear
They make the hay in Dorset Dear.
From early morn till twilight grey
They toss and turn and shake the hay.
And all the countryside is gay
With roses on the fallen may,
For 'tis the hay-time of the year
In Dorset Dear.

The loaded waggons wend their way
Across the pasture-lands, and stay
Beside the hedge where foxgloves peer;
And ricks that shall be fashioned here
Will be the sweetest stuff, they say,
In Dorset Dear!

Fay Inchfawn

THE WIND

WHY does the wind so want to be
    Here in my little room with me?
He's all the world to blow about,
But just because I keep him out
He cannot be a moment still,
But frets upon my window sill,
And sometimes brings a noisy rain
To help him batter at the pane.

Upon my door he comes to knock.
He rattles, rattles at the lock,
And lifts the latch and stirs the key,
Then waits a moment breathlessly,
And soon, more fiercely than before,
He shakes my little trembling door,
And though, " Come in, come in!" I say,
He neither comes nor goes away.

Barefoot across the chilly floor
I run and open wide the door;
He rushes in and back again
He goes to batter door and pane,
Pleased to have blown my candle out.
He's all the world to blow about,
Why does he want so much to be
Here in my little room with me?

                    E. Rendall

A WALK WITH JANE

DREAMY, drowsy, daisy days
      Of summer sun and butterflies,
Of purple vetch and clover leaves,
Of buttercups and dandelions,
And Jane—grass-high and golden-haired.

The hawthorn, sweet and blossom white,
Stretch on before us, mile on mile,
While peacock blue and cabbage white
Dance dizzily from flower to flower
In endless, ageless pas de deux.

The joy sublime of tiny Jane,
Who revels in the simple things,
Like golden flowers and ladybirds,
And shining stones, and tickling grass,
And dandelions that tell the time.

Pat Ashmore

THESE I LOVE

WHITE cottages done with thatch.
   Yellow corn stacks in a batch.
Little chickens when they hatch—
   These I love.

The wind that moans in trees nearby,
Leaves of autumn when they die,
Or new-mown hay where I could lie—
   These I love.

Cowslips, primroses, violets blue,
My little doggie scurrying thro'
Roses caught by morning dew—
   These I love.

The dusty road, or shady lane,
Raindrops on a window pane.
To stroke a horse's glossy mane—
   These I love.

A collie dog with big brown eyes,
A hawk on wing, as homeward hies,
Buzzing bees, and dragonflies—
   These I love.

The church bells' ring at eventide,
A rainbow with its colours pied,
The house in which I now abide—
   These I love.

                    Anonymous

TO THE COMING SPRING

A PUNCTUAL Spring!
    We had forgotten in this winter town
The days of Summer and the long, long eves.
But now you come on airy wing,
With busy fingers spilling baby-leaves
On all the bushes, and a faint green down
On ancient trees, and everywhere
Your warm breath soft with kisses
Stirs the wintry air,
And waking us to unimagined blisses.
Your lightest footprints in the grass
Are marked by painted crocus-flowers
And heavy-headed daffodils,
While little trees blush faintly as you pass.
The morning and the night
You bathe with heavenly showers,
And scatter scentless violets on the rounded hills,
Drop beneath leafless woods pale primrose posies.
With magic key, in the new evening light,
You are unlocking buds that keep the roses;
The purple lilac soon will blow above the wall
And bended boughs in orchards whitely bloom—
We had forgotten in the Winter's gloom . . .
Soon we shall hear the cuckoo call!

Margaret Mackenzie

ROMANCE

STRANGER than dream
    Is twilight deep on the road
Tired men are wending;
The gathering breeze,
Horses, the swaying load
Of the scented hay, the gleam
Red on the trees,
With daylight ending.

Quieter than sleep
Firelight over the wall
In familiar places,
The half-read book,
Mother, the rise and fall
Of the patient thread, the deep
Comforting look
Of the gentle faces.

K. V. Chevis

THE OLD HOUSE

A LITTLE house with sloping floors,
    And ceilings dark with oaken beams,
And wooden latches to the doors—
    A little house all full of dreams.

A twisting stairway ages old,
    A chimney-place so deep and wide
That when the winter wind blows cold
    You may creep close—and sit inside.

A little house right on the street—
    The cobbled street—grown o'er with grass
Where you may hear the ring of feet,
    And singing voice of children pass.

And sometimes for a little space
    My house a storied heart lays bare,
And doth unveil a secret place
    Of memory, intimate and rare . . .

When I, a little wearied grown,
    To my last sleep must go some day,
In dreams my spirit will return—
    It could not bear to be away.

                              M. E. Mason

TWO SCHOOLS

SHE grows dianthus—I grow pinks.
   My larkspur, her delphinium;
A classicist, my neighbour shrinks
From green and non-botanic thumb.

The stately lemon-lily glows
Fainter as hemerocalis,
And velvet foxgloves lose their shape
For me as digitalis.

His daisies pied, his violets blue,
Who sang of Avon's meadows knew
How deeply bred the roots, how dear
The common name to native ear.

Barbarian to my neighbour's eye,
My nomenclature she condemns,
Yet grants my flowers thrive as well
As hers on Greek and Latin stems.

Mary Adams Krauss

SUDDEN LIGHT

I HAVE been here before,
   But when or how I cannot tell:
I know the grass beyond the door,
   The sweet keen smell,
The sighing sound, the lights around the shore.

You have been mine before—
   How long ago I may not know:
But just when at that swallow's soar
   Your neck turned so,
Some veil did fall—I knew it all of yore.

Has this been thus before?
   And shall not thus time's eddying flight
Still with our lives our love restore
   In death's despite,
And day and night yield one delight once more?

D.G. Rossetti

WIND'S WORK

KATE rose up early as fresh as a lark,
  Almost in time to see vanish the dark;
Jack rather later, bouncing from bed,
Saw fade on the dawn's cheek the last flush of red:
Yet who knows
When the wind rose?

Kate went to watch the new lambs at their play
And stroke the white calf born yesterday;
Jack sought the woods where trees grow tall
As who would learn to swarm them all:
Yet who knows
Where the wind goes?

Kate has sown candy-tuft, lupins and peas,
Carnations, forget-me-not and heart's ease;
Jack has sown cherry-pie, marigold,
Love-that-lies-bleeding and snap-dragons bold:
But who knows
What the wind sows?

Kate knows a thing or two useful at home,
Darns like a fairy, and churns like a gnome;
Jack is a wise man at shaping a stick,
Once he's in the saddle the pony may kick.
But hark to the wind how it blows!
None comes, none goes,
None reaps or mows,
No friends turn foes,
No hedge bears sloes,
And no cock crows,
But the wind knows!

T. Sturge Moore

SUMMER DAWN

PRAY but one prayer for me 'twixt thy closed
   lips,
Think but one thought of me up in the stars.
The summer night waneth, the morning light slips
Faint and grey 'twixt the leaves of the aspen,
   betwixt the cloud bars,
That are patiently waiting there for the dawn:
Patient and colourless, though Heaven's gold
Waits to float through them along with the sun.

Far out in the meadows, above the young corn,
The heavy elms wait, and restless and cold
The uneasy wind rises; the roses are dun;
Through the long twilight they pray for the dawn,
Round the lone house in the midst of the corn,
Speak but one word to me over the corn,
Over the tender, bow'd locks of the corn.

William Mortis

INTERRUPTIONS

"I WISH," said Susan, " when I play pretending,
    When I'm a knight, a hero, or a queen,
They wouldn't say, ' Your overall needs mending!'
    They wouldn't say, ' Your hands are never
        clean!' "

" I wish, I wish," said Susan, " when I'm sitting
    Proudly as Helen by the shores of Greece,
They wouldn't say, ' Oh, Susan, fetch my knitting—
    I left it on the nursery mantelpiece!' "

" I wish," said Susan, " when I find a casket
    Brimming with gold and jewels of the crown,
They wouldn't say, ' That's Granny's mending-
        basket,
    I told you not to touch it. Put it down!' "

" I wish," said Susan, " when the shadows flicker,
    And I and all my merry men have supped,
And in the shrubbery the trees seem thicker,
    I wish, I wish they wouldn't interrupt!' "

Barbara Euphan Todd

SPRING SONG

DARK clouds on a white sky
  And the rough north wind blowing;
Bare trees in a brown land
By a full river flowing.
    Melting snow,
    Sweet earth below,
And the first green buds showing.

White clouds on a blue sky
And the April days flying;
Bird song in the green woods
And the young lambs crying.
    Dancing hours,
    Fresh nodding flowers,
And the young ploughman sighing.

Bright kites on a windy hill
And the far church bells ringing;
Old wives in the sunshine
And a shepherd singing.
    Furrowing ploughs,
    White apple boughs,
And a gay skylark springing.

Alan Temperley

THE PASSIONATE SHEPHERD
TO HIS LOVE

COME live with me and be my love,
  And we will all the pleasures prove,
That hills and valleys, dales and fields,
And all the craggy mountains yields.

There we will sit upon the rocks,
And see the shepherds feed their flocks,
By shallow rivers to whose falls
Melodious birds sing madrigals.

And I will make thee beds of roses
With a thousand fragrant posies,
A cap of flowers, and a kirtle
Embroidered all with leaves or myrtle;

A gown made of the finest wool
Which from our pretty lambs we pull;
Fair lined slippers for the cold,
With buckles of the purest gold;

A belt of straw and ivy buds,
With coral clasps and amber studs:
And if these pleasures may thee move,
Come live with me and be my love.

The shepherds' swains shall dance and sing
For thy delight each May morning:
If these delights thy mind may move,
Then live with me and be my love.

Christopher Marlowe

NIGHT IN THE GARDEN

I KNOW that I am growing old
　　And to a mounting tally add my days,
But still I find that life is sweet
　　For memory past time repays
And spreads lost dreams about my feet.

And still for me on nights like this
　　The stars sing all together in the sky,
While flowers and trees enchanted stand
　　To hear such music swell and die
Across the bright moon-painted land.

The years turn fast and faster still,
　　They steal my joys and all my youth away,
But memory holds wide the door
　　And bids each cherished moment stay
With me and make me young once more.

Mary C. Marshall

THE BEST DAYS

OUR children's children love to call
  To climb a tree or scale a wall,
They like fresh baked drop scones for tea
And love to sit on Grandad's knee;
They chase and catch the butterflies
Then study them with avid eyes
Or play for hours with matchbox toys—
The ones their fathers had when boys.

And when, sometimes, they stay the night
Pyjama clad and tucked up tight
We view them fast asleep in bed
And dearly love each tousled head;
Each moment holds a memory
Of how *our* children used to be
Yes, they're the brightest days of all—
The days our children's children call!

Mary M. Milne

GIPSY-LURE

TODAY I'll go a-gipsying,
   The leafy lanes are calling,
And dream away a happy day
   From morn to twilight's falling.

The dew is on the meadow grass,
   The wind is in the clover.
Haste, laggard feet! the day is sweet,
   And summer's nearly over.

What lies beyond the white road's bend?
   Adventure bids me follow,
My heart's desire a gipsy fire
   Down in some warm green hollow.

My heart craves sight of a wild flower,
   Not those on hawkers' barrows;
I have not heard for days a bird
   But chirping city sparrows.

Too long I have been cramped in town,
   The weeks like ages seeming.
Haste, weary feet! Now time is fleet,
   A day's too short for dreaming.

Winifred Williams

ON A GOLD AND PURPLE DAY

IN my little cottage garden,
    A patchwork quilt of every hue,
I like to sit awhile and savour
    Jewels wrought by sun and dew;
Drinking in the honeyed sweetness—
    Leisurely the while I may—
Of the mellow autumn sunshine,
    On a gold and purple day.

In my rather crowded garden,
    Tall hollyhocks in bright array
Chat with regal blue delphiniums,
    Crimson creeper trails its way
Along the cracked uneven flagstones,
    Climbs the walls and old stone porch,
Betimes to glow in moth-winged twilight
    Vividly as flaring torch.

In my lovely fragrant garden,
    A home for every passing bee,
I rather like the tangled beauty
    No-one knows as well as me.
Pimpernels—I can't destroy them,
    They find favour in my eyes,
As do little heart's-ease pansies;
    Tho' of course, it might be wise.

In the sanctum of my garden,
    Wildling blooms shall find retreat;
And why should I my soft heart harden
    (Ruminating from my seat)
If they're beautiful they're staying—
    Heedless I'll not care a hoot
What old friends and neighbours frown on,
    Things there are one can't uproot!

Violet Hall

THE HOUSE OF GHOSTS

FIRST to describe the house. Who has not seen it
 once at the end of an evening's walk—the
  leaves
that suddenly open, and as sudden screen it
 with the first flickering hint of shadowy eaves?

Was there a light in the high window? Or
 only the moon's cool candle palely lit?
Was there a pathway leading to the door?
 Or only grass and none to walk on it?

And surely someone cried, " Who goes there—
 who?"
 And ere the lips could shape the whispered " I,"
the same voice rose, and chuckled, " You, 'tis you!"
 A voice, or the furred night-owl's human cry?

Who has not seen the house? Who has not started
 towards the gate half-seen, and paused, half-
  fearing,
and half beyond all fear—and the leaves parted
 again, and there was nothing in the clearing?

       Humbert Wolfe

THE GOLDFINCH

SWEET little bird with a red satin face
  Poised on a thistle with infinite grace,
Daffodil-yellow the flash on his wing,
Feathers all perfect as jewels in a ring.

We watched from the window in breathless delight
For an exquisite moment, and then he took flight.
I turned from the window my spirits downcast,
He came not again—'twas too lovely to last.

" Look, Mummy, look!" cried my five-year-old son,
" A picture of Goldie, the very same one!
I've bought with my sixpence, dear Mummy, and so
You can have your own goldfinch wherever you go!"

Thirty years have gone by since that long-ago day,
Many things have been lost or have vanished away,
But the picture still hangs at the side of my bed.
The bird's gem-bright colours of yellow and red
Have faded a little, but I can yet see
My son's happy face as he gave it to me.

Rosemary Glubb

FABLE

WHERE the white lane meets with the green
    The year's first butterflies are seen;
Here settling upon leaf or stone,
They spread their colours in the sun.

This is the chosen trysting place
Of butterflies' whole painted race;
Hither the gentle, favouring wind
Of Spring shall bring to each his kind.

See, ever full of hope and love,
The basker leap to her above
At the first brushing of her shadow—
Over the hedge, across the meadow!

But ah, how fortune mocks delight!
The tortoiseshell pursues the white,
The yellow brimstone tracks the shade,
Zig-zag, the splendid peacock made.

Swiftly the fair day droops and dies
Above unmated butterflies;
Again, again, and yet again,
Comes the wrong lover down the lane.

Though still deceived they still return
To wait, to hope, perchance to mourn.
Alas! poor fools, how must they rue
Who but a flickering shade pursue!

Happier we and wiser far
Than these misguided insects are,
For whom both love and life are lost
At the first touch of evening frost.

Sylvia Lynd

THE LATE, LAST ROOK

THE old gilt vane and spire receive
  The last beam eastward striking;
The first shy bat to peep at eve
  Has found her to his liking.
The Western heaven is dull and grey,
The last red glow has followed day.

The late, last rook is housed and will
  With cronies lie till to-morrow;
If there's a rook loquacious still
  In dream he hunts a furrow,
And flaps behind a spectre team,
Or ghostly scarecrows walk his dream.

Ralph Hodgson

ACKNOWLEDGMENTS

Our thanks to the Society of Authors as the literary representative of the Estate of John Masefield for "On Eastnor Knoll" by John Masefield; to the Literary Trustees of Walter de la Mare and the Society of Authors for "The Linnet" and "All That's Past"; to The Society of Authors and Miss Pamela Hinkson for "My Hearth" by Katharine Tynan; to Macmillan, London and Basingstoke, for "Fable" by Sylvia Lynd; to Fudge and Co., Ltd., for "The Expedition" and "The Goldfinch" by Rosemary Glubb; to Charles Griffiths for "Windfalls in the Moonlight" by Aileen E. Passmore; to Kate Bone for "Invitation"; to Mary Marshall for "Lonely Places" and "Night In The Garden"; to Marion Elliot for "Goodnight"; to Pat Ashmore for "A Walk With Jane"; to Alan Temperley for "Spring Song"; to Mary M. Milne for "The Best Days"; to Winifred Williams for "Gipsy Lure"; to Violet Hall for "On A Gold And Purple Day".